Essential COOKING SERIES

COMPREHENSIVE, STEP BY STEP COOKING

Chicken Meals

HINKLER
BOOKS

Food Editor: Ellen Argyriou
Project Editor: Lara Morcombe
Design: Studio Pazzo
Cover Design: Hinkler Books Studio

Essential Cooking Series: Chicken Meals
First published in 2005 by Hinkler Books Pty Ltd
45-55 Fairchild Street
Heatherton, Victoria 3202 Australia
www.hinklerbooks.com

Disclaimer: The nutritional information listed under each recipe does not
include the nutrient content of garnishes or any accompaniments not listed
in specific quantitites in the ingredient list. The nutritional information for
each recipe is an estimate only, and may vary depending on the brand of
ingredients used, and due to natural biological variations in the composition
of natural foods such as meat, fish, fruit and vegetables. The nutritional
information was calculated by using Foodworks dietary analysis software
(Version 3, Xyris Software Pty Ltd, Highgate Hill, Queensland, Australia) based
on the Australian food composition tables and food manufacturers' data.
Where not specified, ingredients are always analysed as average or medium,
not small or large.

ISBN- 13:978-1-7412-1938-8

Printed and bound in China

10 9 8 7 6 5
10 09 08 07

Contents

An introduction to chicken meals

A whole chicken, chicken cuts, mince, stir-fry pieces, casserole pieces and even chicken bones to make stock are readily available in the market place, making chicken the number one home-cooked fast food.

From a quick stir-fry or grill to a roasted chicken dinner or tasty casserole, chicken can be cooked and served in a great variety of ways.

NUTRITIONAL VALUE

- It's rich in protein containing all of the 8 essential amino acids.

- Vitamins are well represented, particularly vitamins A and B. Iron, phosphorus and zinc are also present.

- It's low in fat, particularly when the skin is removed.

- It's tender to eat and easy to digest making it especially suited for infants, children and the elderly.

PURCHASING AND STORAGE TIPS

Fresh chicken

- Make it the last purchase on your shopping trip. Place the chicken in an insulated bag to keep it cold on the trip home.

- Refrigerate the chicken immediately after you arrive home. Remove it from the package, rinse and pat dry. Place in a dish and cover loosely with plastic wrap. Place in the coldest part of the refrigerator, below 4°C (39°F). It may be kept for 3 days. Treat chicken pieces in the same way.

- If chicken needs to be stored longer, it is better to buy ready frozen chicken than to buy fresh and freeze at home.

- If the chicken pieces are to be purchased and frozen for future use, make sure they are fresh and not previously frozen. Wipe dry with paper towel then pack flat in plastic freezer bags. Extract air by pushing out towards the opening, and tape the bag closed. Label and date packages.

Frozen chicken

- Make sure the chicken is frozen solid and that there are no signs of a torn package and no ice deposits in the base of the package. This is a sign of partial thaw and refreezing which may result in a higher bacterial count in the chicken.

- Place in the freezer immediately on arrival home.

- Thaw frozen chicken thoroughly before cooking to avoid toughening the texture and to reduce the chance of some parts being undercooked. Under-cooked parts could harbour food-spoiling bacteria.

- Do not refreeze thawed chicken. It is advisable to cook the thawed chicken and freeze it when cooked if necessary.

- To thaw a frozen chicken, remove it from the wrap and place it on a rack in a dish to allow liquid to collect beneath the chicken. Cover loosely with plastic wrap and place in the refrigerator for 24 hours. This is the safest way to thaw. Thawing on the kitchen bench must be avoided for bacterial growth may commence on the top area first thawed. Thawing in the microwave is quick and safe, but remember to follow the manufacturer's instructions.

PREPARATION FOR COOKING

Whole chickens for roasting

Scrape inside the cavity with a fork to release the remaining giblets. Rinse under running water inside and out. Pat dry inside and out with paper towels. You may rub the chicken inside and out with half a lemon, squeezing out juice as you rub. It gives the chicken a delightful fresh flavour.

To truss a chicken

Cut a piece of kitchen string long enough to encircle the chicken twice. Pin back the wings and insert a skewer through the body under the legs and through to the other side. Pick up the string at its centre and loop around the parson's nose (tail). Holding the string in each hand loop around the drumstick ends then cross over pulling the legs together. Loop around the skewer at each side, then take the string along the sides and loop around the wings. Turn the chicken over and tie. Trussing keeps the chicken in shape while roasting.

FOR SMALL CHICKENS: Loop string around parson's nose, cross over then loop around each drumstick and pull together and tie.

Chicken breast fillets

PAN-FRIED BREAST FILLETS: It is best to have an even thickness to ensure even contact with the base of the hot pan. Place the fillet between 2 sheets of plastic wrap and pound the higher centre lightly with the side of a meat mallet or a rolling pin until the thickness evens out.

Chicken schnitzel

A thinner fillet is needed. Pound as above but with outward strokes to extend the fillet outwards making it thinner.

Thigh fillets

The bone and skin have been removed. These fillets may be used for pan frying, for schnitzels or pounded out very thinly and formed into rolls with stuffing. It is best to slit the white membrane on the shiny side of the fillet in several places with a small pointed knife. This will allow the fillet to stretch and flatten as it is pounded. Proceed as for chicken fillets above.

Chicken wings

Wings may be cooked whole or joints separated. For whole wings turn the wing tip behind the end joint to form an attractive triangular shape.

To make mini drumsticks

Use the first joint of the wing which has a meaty bulb at the end. Hold the end of the bone firmly; with a small sharp knife scrape the flesh around the bone towards and almost to the top end. Push the meat over the end to form a small drumstick. Marinate and grill for finger food.

HANDY COOKING TIPS

1 To roast chicken with a crisp skin: Place the washed chicken in the refrigerator uncovered for 2 hours. The cold air dries the skin which when roasted becomes crisp and tasty.

2 Boneless chicken breast fillets are very tender and will toughen if overcooked. Cook for 3–4 minutes each side under a preheated grill. Brushing with a little oil or a marinade before cooking will keep the fillets juicy and tender.

Thicker pieces of chicken such as half breast with bone and skin, Maryland pieces or drumsticks and thighs need lower heat and longer cooking time to allow the heat to penetrate into the centre. Place the grill tray in a lower position to be further away from the heat. Cook for 5–8 minutes each side or longer if very thick, then move the grill tray closer to the heat to brown and crisp for final cooking. Pierce the chicken with a skewer, if juices run clear the chicken is ready. If they are a pink colour more cooking is needed.

3 Barbecued chicken drumsticks are often served blackened on the outside and rare in the centre. Never serve rare chicken as the bacteria which may be present will not have been destroyed. To cook properly, place the chicken on the cooler part of the barbecue, or on a wire rack raised above the heat. Cook for 20–25 minutes turning occasionally to allow heat to penetrate to the centre, then place directly onto the hot grill bars for 5 minutes to brown and crisp, turning frequently.

4 Chicken pieces for cooking in a simmer sauce must be first browned all over to seal in the juices. Heat a little oil in a suitable saucepan and brown a few pieces at a time. Remove then add the next batch. If the pan is crowded the temperature will drop, juices will be extracted and browning prevented. Drain the fat from the pan before adding the simmer sauce. Bring quickly to the boil, turn down to a simmer and return the browned chicken to the pan. Simmer for 35–40 minutes to cook the chicken to the bone.

5 To poach chicken breasts for use in cold dishes, salads, and sandwich and focaccia fillings: Place chicken in a saucepan, add a piece of onion, celery, carrot, salt and a few peppercorns. Pour over enough hot water to almost cover and bring to a simmer, cover and simmer slowly for 20–25 minutes until tender. Allow to cool in the liquid; reserve the stock for other use. Whole fresh chicken may be poached in the same way for 30–35 minutes. When cool remove the skin and carefully ease the chicken flesh from the bones.

TO JOINT A CHICKEN

It is more economical to cut a whole chicken into pieces yourself than to buy ready cut pieces. Use a large sharp knife and a chopping board.

1 Place chicken on its back with legs towards you. Pull the left leg away from the body and cut through the skin to expose the joint. Bend the leg backwards at the joint to dislocate it. Cut through the joint to free the leg. Turn chicken

around and remove the other leg. If you wish to separate the drumstick from the thigh locate the joint and cut through.

2 To remove the breast cut through the flap of skin on each side and continue to cut through the fine rib bones until you meet resistance from stronger bones. Gently chop through these bones to the neck on both sides and cut free of the backbone.

3 To divide the whole breast, place skin side down and press to open out wide. Lay the carving knife along the line of white cartilage, press down hard or hit the back of the knife with a meat mallet to insert it into the cartilage, then cut through to separate the 2 sides. The wings may be removed at the main joint next to the breast or cut off at the second joint. Each breast may be cut into 2 portions if desired.

Vindaloo chicken nuggets

INGREDIENTS

1 kg (2 lb) chicken thigh fillets
salt and pepper
1 tablespoon lemon juice
2 tablespoons vindaloo curry paste
125 g (4 oz) flour
2 eggs, lightly beaten
185 g (6½ oz) dried breadcrumbs
canola oil spray
yoghurt and cucumber
  dipping sauce
1 lebanese cucumber, grated
1 cup (250 g, 8 oz) plain yoghurt
1 clove garlic, crushed
1 tablespoon lemon juice
salt and pepper to taste
makes 32

PREPARATION TIME
20 minutes, plus
2 hours marinating

COOKING TIME
15–18 minutes

1 Cut each thigh fillet into 4 pieces. In a bowl, place fillets and sprinkle lightly with salt and pepper. Pour over 1 tablespoon lemon juice. Toss to mix through. Rub the vindaloo curry paste well into each piece with your fingers. Cover and refrigerate 2 hours or more.

2 Preheat oven to 200°C (400°F, gas mark 6). Into shallow dishes or trays, place the flour, egg and breadcrumbs. Coat the chicken nuggets in flour, dip into the egg and press into the breadcrumbs to coat all sides. Lightly spray a large flat tray with canola oil spray. Place nuggets on the tray and spray the tops. Cook in a preheated oven for 15–18 minutes.

3 Into a strainer, place the cucumber and press to drain off excess liquid. Mix into the yoghurt. Add garlic, lemon juice, salt and pepper and place in a serving bowl. Serve with the hot nuggets.

NUTRITIONAL VALUE PER SERVE   FAT 5.7 G   CARBOHYDRATE 12.4 G   PROTEIN 15 G

Chicken and almond triangles

INGREDIENTS

1 tablespoon olive oil
60 g (2 oz) slivered almonds
1 medium onion, finely
   chopped
$1/2$ teaspoon salt
1 teaspoon ground cinnamon
1 teaspoon paprika
2 teaspoons ground cumin
500 g (1 lb) chicken mince
2 small tomatoes, chopped
45 g (1 $1/2$ oz) raisins, chopped
2 tablespoons finely
   chopped flat-leaf parsley
4 tablespoons dry white wine
14 sheets filo pastry
canola oil spray
makes 42

1 Heat a heavy-based frying pan. Add a teaspoon of the oil and sauté the almonds until pale gold in colour. Quickly remove with a slotted spoon. Add remaining oil and the onion and fry until soft. Stir in salt, cinnamon, paprika and cumin and cook until aromatic. Add chicken mince and stir-fry until almost cooked. Add tomatoes, raisins, parsley, wine and cooked almonds. Simmer covered for 15 minutes. Uncover and cook until juices are absorbed. Allow to cool.

2 Position pastry with long side in front of you. Cut into 3 even 13.5 cm wide strips. Stack and cover with clean tea towel. Take 2 strips at a time, spray each lightly with canola oil spray and fold in half, long side to long side. Spray surface with oil spray.

3 Place a teaspoon of filling on bottom end of each strip. Fold right-hand corner over to form a triangle then fold on the straight then on diagonal until end is reached. Repeat with remaining. Place on a tray sprayed with oil. Spray tops of triangles with oil and bake in a preheated moderate oven for 20–25 minutes. Serve hot as finger food.

PREPARATION TIME
30 minutes

COOKING TIME
48 minutes

NUTRITIONAL VALUE PER SERVE	FAT 8.6 G	CARBOHYDRATE 12.2 G	PROTEIN 10.6 G

Lavish rolls

INGREDIENTS

1 kg (2 lb) chicken tenderloins
1 packet of 8 lavash flat breads
340 g (11½ oz) jar mayonnaise
1 small lettuce, shredded
½ bunch spring onions (green onions), chopped
4 tomatoes, sliced
other vegetables of choice, eg., avocado, carrot (optional)
250 g (8 oz) tub of hummus
2 tablespoons lemon juice
serves 8

1 Spray a heated non-stick pan or grill plate with oil spray and cook tenderloins for 2 minutes on each side.

2 Place in turn each lavash sheet on work surface. Spread lightly with mayonnaise. Sprinkle with shredded lettuce leaving the bottom 4 cm uncovered. Sprinkle spring onions over the lettuce and place on tomato slices and other vegetables. Place 3–4 tenderloins down the centre and drizzle with a little hummus thinned down with lemon juice.

3 Turn up bottom edge to hold in the filling and roll from the side into a tight roll. Wrap bottom half in greaseproof paper or foil and serve.

PREPARATION TIME
20 minutes

COOKING TIME
4 minutes

NUTRITIONAL VALUE PER SERVE	FAT 7.5 G	CARBOHYDRATE 11.7 G	PROTEIN 8.8 G

Chicken focaccia with marinated vegetables

INGREDIENTS

500 g (1 lb) chicken breast fillets
1 clove garlic, crushed
salt and pepper to taste
1 tablespoon lemon juice
2 teaspoons olive oil
6 portions of focaccia bread
  either individual or slab
1 tablespoon olive oil
6 slices marinated roasted
  eggplant (aubergine)
100 g (3½ oz) marinated mushrooms
6 slices marinated roasted
  red capsicum (pepper)
serves 6

1 In a non-metallic dish, place chicken breast fillets and add garlic, salt, pepper, lemon juice and oil. Cover and marinate for 30 minutes in the refrigerator. Heat a non-stick pan or greased grill plate and sear the fillets for 1 minute on each side. Cook a further 2 minutes on each side. When cooked cut into diagonal slices. Keep hot.

2 Cut the focaccia slab into serving portions and split through the centre. Brush cut surface with olive oil. Place a slice of eggplant on each base, arrange chicken slices on top and cover with mushrooms and capsicums. Replace top slice. Place in a moderate oven at 160°C (325°F, gas mark 3) to heat for 10 minutes. Serve hot.

PREPARATION TIME
8 minutes, plus
30 minutes marinating

COOKING TIME
7–8 minutes

NUTRITIONAL VALUE PER SERVE	FAT 4.6 G	CARBOHYDRATE 19.3 G	PROTEIN 10.1 G

Chicken yakitori

INGREDIENTS

500 g (1 lb) chicken tenderloins
4 tablespoons teriyaki sauce
4 tablespoons honey
1 clove garlic, crushed
¼ teaspoon ground ginger
4 bamboo skewers, soaked
oil for greasing
makes 15-20

1 In a non-metallic bowl, place chicken. In a separate bowl, combine teriyaki sauce, honey, garlic and ginger. Pour over chicken. Cover and place in refrigerator to marinate for several hours or overnight.

2 Thread 1 or 2 tenderloins onto each skewer, using weaving motion. Heat barbeque or electric grill to medium-high. Grease grill bars lightly with oil.

3 Place skewers in a row and cook for 2 minutes on each side, brushing with marinade as they cook and when turned. Remove to a large plate. Serve immediately as finger food.

PREPARATION TIME
10 minutes, plus several hours or overnight marinating

COOKING TIME
4–5 minutes

NUTRITIONAL VALUE PER SERVE	FAT 5.3 G	CARBOHYDRATE 15.8 G	PROTEIN 15.2 G

Chicken party sticks

INGREDIENTS

500 g (2 lb) chicken tenderloins
salt and pepper to taste
2 packets frozen puff pastry sheets
1 cup (250 ml, 8 fl oz) of bottled
  satay or sweet chilli sauce
2 tablespoons milk
1 tablespoon poppy or sesame seeds
makes 32

1 Preheat oven to 180°C (350°F, gas mark 4).
Sprinkle salt and pepper over the chicken. Cut
sheet of thawed pastry into 4 squares. Place a
chicken tenderloin on each square and add a
dash of your chosen sauce. Roll up on the
diagonal, leaving ends open. Place seam-side
down on a flat oven tray and glaze with milk.
Sprinkle with poppy or sesame seeds.

2 Bake in preheated oven for 25–30 minutes.
Serve hot as finger food with same sauce used
as a dipping sauce.

PREPARATION TIME
15 minutes

COOKING TIME
25–30 minutes

NUTRITIONAL VALUE PER SERVE   FAT **18.3** G   CARBOHYDRATE **25.2** G   PROTEIN **9.2** G

Spicy chicken burritos

INGREDIENTS

500 g (1 lb) chicken stir-fry
1 tablespoon olive oil
1 large onion, finely chopped
1 clove garlic, crushed
180 g (6 oz) tomato
    and garlic pasta sauce
1/2 teaspoon chilli powder
1 packet of 12 Mexican tortillas
topping
1 tub guacamole
2 large onions, thinly sliced
1 carton sour cream
350 g (11 1/2 oz) cheddar cheese,
    grated
420 g (14 oz) can refried beans,
    heated (optional)
makes 32

1 Chop the stir-fry into smaller pieces. Heat the oil in a large frying pan. Add onions and garlic and fry until soft. Add the chicken and stir to brown on all sides. Stir in tomato pasta sauce and chilli powder. Simmer for 15 minutes or until chicken is cooked and sauce thickens.

2 Prepare the toppings and place in suitable serving dishes. Heat a large frying pan, place in a tortilla and heat for 40 seconds on each side. Remove and place on a clean towel and cover. Heat remainder and stack in towel.

3 On each tortilla spread a portion of chicken mixture and top with toppings of choice. Roll up and serve immediately.

PREPARATION TIME
10 minutes

COOKING TIME
18 minutes

NUTRITIONAL VALUE PER SERVE	FAT 11.4 G	CARBOHYDRATE 7.6 G	PROTEIN 9.5 G

Char-grilled chicken with mango salsa

INGREDIENTS

4 chicken breast fillets
2 tablespoons Thai fish sauce
juice of ½ lime
salt and black pepper
1 tablespoon olive oil
fresh mint to garnish
lime wedges to serve
salsa
½ red capsicum (pepper),
   deseeded and quartered
1 mango, chopped
1 small red chilli, deseeded
   and finely chopped
1 tablespoon olive oil
juice of ½ lime
1 tablespoon chopped
   fresh coriander
1 tablespoon chopped fresh mint
salt and pepper
serves 4

1 Place the chicken breasts between cling film and pound with a rolling pin to flatten them slightly. Unwrap and place in a non-metallic dish. In a small bowl, combine the fish sauce, lime juice, salt and pepper and pour over the chicken. Cover and leave to marinate in the refrigerator for 1 hour.

2 Preheat the grill to high. Grill the capsicum skin side up until it blisters. Peel off the skin and dice. In a bowl, combine the mango, capsicum, chilli, oil, lime juice, coriander, mint, salt and pepper. Cover and refrigerate.

3 Heat the tablespoon of oil in a large heavy-based frying pan. Add the chicken and fry for 3–4 minutes on each side. Pour over any remaining marinade and cook until chicken is cooked through. Remove to a serving plate. Serve with mango salsa and garnish with mint and lime.

PREPARATION TIME
20 minutes, plus
1 hour marinating

COOKING TIME
20 minutes

NUTRITIONAL VALUE PER SERVE   FAT 6.3 G   CARBOHYDRATE 1.8 G   PROTEIN 16.9 G

Grilled sesame chicken with ginger rice

INGREDIENTS

500 (1 lb) chicken tenderloin
soy and honey marinade
1 tablespoon sesame seeds, toasted
1 tablespoon rice wine (mirin)
  or sherry
2 teaspoons honey or plum sauce
2 teaspoons soy sauce
2 teaspoons oyster sauce
1 teaspoon sesame oil
ginger rice
1 tablespoon finely chopped
  fresh ginger
1 teaspoon sesame oil
1 cup (220 g, 7½ oz) short-grain rice,
  rinsed and drained
330 ml (11 fl oz) ginger beer
1 tablespoon pickled or
  preserved ginger
1 spring onion (green onion),
  finely chopped
serves 4

1 In a non-metallic bowl, place sesame seeds, wine, honey, soy and oyster sauces and sesame oil. Mix to combine. Add chicken and toss to coat. Cover and marinate in the refrigerator for at least 1 hour.

2 Place fresh ginger and sesame oil in a large saucepan over a low heat. Cook, stirring occasionally, for 5 minutes. Add rice. Cook, stirring, for 2 minutes. Stir in ginger beer and pickled ginger. Bring to the boil. Reduce heat and cover. Simmer for 10–15 minutes or until liquid is absorbed and rice is cooked. Stir in spring onion.

3 Preheat grill or barbecue to a medium heat. Lightly oil the grill bars and place on the tenderloins. Cook for 3–4 minutes on each side, brushing regularly with marinade. Serve chicken with ginger rice.

PREPARATION TIME
5 minutes

COOKING TIME
25 minutes

NUTRITIONAL VALUE PER SERVE	FAT 2.6 G	CARBOHYDRATE 30 G	PROTEIN 3 G

Spicy satay skewers

INGREDIENTS

500 g (1 lb) thigh fillets
salt and pepper
1 tablespoon lemon juice
1 clove garlic, crushed
satay sauce
180 g (6 fl oz) peanut butter
$^3/_4$ cup (180 ml, 6 fl oz) water
2 tablespoons brown sugar
$^1/_8$ teaspoon chilli powder,
   or to taste
1 tablespoon soy sauce
1 tablespoon grated onion
2 tablespoons toasted
   sesame seeds
bamboo skewers, soaked
serves 4–5

1 Mix all satay sauce ingredients together in a saucepan, heat to simmer, then simmer for 5 minutes. Remove from heat and allow to cool.

2 Cut thigh fillets in half down the centre. Cut the thinner side into 2 and the thicker side into 3 pieces. Place in a bowl and sprinkle with salt, pepper, lemon juice and garlic, stir to mix through. Pour marinade over chicken, cover and stand to marinate in the refrigerator for at least 1 hour or leave overnight in the refrigerator.

3 Soak bamboo skewers in water. Thread 4–5 pieces onto each skewer until just touching. If pushed too close together, the centre will not cook sufficiently.

4 Grill or barbecue on moderately high heat for 10–12 minutes turning frequently and brushing with sauce. Remove to platter and sprinkle with toasted sesame seeds. Serve with remaining satay sauce.

PREPARATION TIME
8 minutes, plus
1 hour or overnight
marinating

COOKING TIME
15 minutes

NUTRITIONAL VALUE PER SERVE   FAT 17.8 G   CARBOHYDRATE 5.5 G   PROTEIN 18.8 G

Chicken waldorf

INGREDIENTS

400 g (13 oz) chicken breast fillets
1 onion, roughly chopped
1 carrot, roughly chopped
pinch of salt
2 red apples
1 tablespoon lemon juice
2 sticks celery, diced
60 g (2 oz) blonde walnuts,
   coarsely chopped
125 g (4 oz) mayonnaise
1 lettuce, separated into cups,
   washed and crisped
serves 6–8

PREPARATION TIME
10 minutes

COOKING TIME
20 minutes

1 To poach the chicken fillets: place fillets, onion, carrot and salt in a
pan and add hot water just to cover. Bring to a simmer, reduce
heat and simmer gently for 20 minutes. Turn off heat and cool in
its juices. Strain, reserve stock for future use.

2 Cut chicken into 1 cm cubes. Wash apples well, leave skin on and
cut into 1 cm cubes. Sprinkle with lemon juice.

3 In a bowl, toss chicken, apples, celery and walnuts together. Add
mayonnaise and gently toss through. Spoon into the lettuce cups
and serve as an entrée or light lunch; or line a salad bowl with
lettuce leaves and pile salad into the centre and serve for a buffet.

NUTRITIONAL VALUE PER SERVE   FAT 6.3 G   CARBOHYDRATE 4.5 G   PROTEIN 6.2 G

Chicken and endive salad with creamy dressing

INGREDIENTS

1 slender French bread stick
(baguette)
1 clove garlic, crushed
2 tablespoons oil
1 bunch curly endive
4 spring onions (green onions), sliced
250 g (8 oz) can mandarin segments,
drained and juice reserved
250 g (8 oz) chicken tenderloins
dressing
250 ml (8 fl oz) coleslaw dressing
1 teaspoon dijon mustard
serves 4

PREPARATION TIME
10 minutes

COOKING TIME
10 minutes

1 Cut bread stick into ½ cm slices. Mix garlic and oil together and brush onto bread slices. Place on a tray in oven and cook at 180°C (350°F, gas mark 4) until crisp and golden. Break endive into 5 cm pieces. In a bowl, toss together endive, spring onions and mandarin segments.

2 Cook tenderloins in a lightly greased non-stick pan for 2 minutes on each side. Mound the bread and endive salad onto individual serving plates and arrange chicken on top. Combine coleslaw dressing and mustard and drizzle over the salad. Serve as an entrée.

NUTRITIONAL VALUE PER SERVE   FAT **9.1** G   CARBOHYDRATE **22.6** G   PROTEIN **6.5** G

Tossed greens and chicken with blue cheese dressing

INGREDIENTS

1 bunch rocket leaves
1 coral lettuce
1 mignonette lettuce
1 red apple, cored, thinly sliced,
   splashed with lemon juice
60 g (2 oz) pale walnut pieces
2 poached chicken breasts
60 g (2 oz) extra blue-vein cheese
   for topping

dressing
4 tablespoons olive oil
2 tablespoons white-wine vinegar
1 tablespoon lemon juice
¼ teaspoon sugar
1 tablespoon dijon mustard
30 g (1 oz) blue-vein cheese,
   crumbled
pinch cayenne

serves 4–6

PREPARATION TIME
15 minutes

1 Wash greens, drain and shake in a tea towel to dry. Tear leaves into pieces and place into a large bowl. Toss in apple slices and half of the walnuts.

2 Cut the chicken into diagonal slices and add to salad greens. Whisk the dressing ingredients together and pour over salad. Sprinkle top with remaining walnuts and extra crumbled blue-vein cheese. Serve as an entrée or luncheon dish.

NUTRITIONAL VALUE PER SERVE   FAT **10.5** G   CARBOHYDRATE **1.9** G   PROTEIN **6.5** G

Curried chicken salad

INGREDIENTS

1 large cooked barbecued chicken
2 sticks celery, finely chopped
6 spring onions (green onions), sliced
60 g (2 oz) raisins, soaked
60 g (2 oz) slivered almonds, toasted
200 g (7 oz) mixed salad greens,
  washed and crisped
1 mango, sliced to garnish
2 tablespoons shredded coconut,
  toasted to garnish
dressing
150 g (5 oz) mayonnaise
150 g (5 oz) low-fat yoghurt
3 tablespoons sweet mango chutney
1 tablespoon mild curry paste
2 tablespoons lemon juice
2 teaspoons freshly grated
  lemon rind
serves 8

PREPARATION TIME
10 minutes, plus
2 hours refrigeration

1 Remove the chicken meat from the bones and cut into bite-size pieces. Toss with the celery, spring onions, raisins and almonds.

2 In a bowl, place all dressing ingredients and whisk until smooth. Pour over chicken, toss to mix through. Cover and chill 2 hours or more.

3 Line platter or individual plates with salad greens and pile on the chicken mixture. Garnish with mango slices and sprinkle with toasted, shredded coconut.

NUTRITIONAL VALUE PER SERVE   FAT **9.1** G   CARBOHYDRATE **7.2** G   PROTEIN **10.3** G

Marinated chicken salad

INGREDIENTS

2 cups (500 ml, 16 fl oz) oil
500 g (1 lb) chicken stir-fry
60 g (2 oz) seasoned flour
4 tablespoons orange juice
4 tablespoons olive oil
1 tablespoon chopped mint
$\frac{1}{2}$ teaspoon salt
freshly ground black pepper
1 avocado, sliced
425 g (14 oz) can apricots
1 punnet snow pea sprouts
serves 6–8

PREPARATION TIME
10 minutes, plus
30 minutes marinating

COOKING TIME
5 minutes

1 Heat oil in a deep frying pan. Dip the stir-fry strips in the seasoned flour a few at a time and deep-fry in the hot oil until cooked and golden in colour. Drain on absorbent paper and place in a glass bowl.

2 Combine orange juice, oil, mint, salt and pepper in a screw-top jar and shake well. Pour over chicken strips and refrigerate for a minimum of 30 minutes.

3 Slice avocado and drain apricot halves, reserving 2 tablespoons of juice from the can. Arrange snow pea sprouts on individual plates. Top with chicken strips, avocado pieces and apricot halves. Add about 1–2 teaspoons juice to remaining marinade and drizzle over salad. Serve as an entrée or as a luncheon dish with crusty bread.

NUTRITIONAL VALUE PER SERVE   FAT 15 G   CARBOHYDRATE 6.4 G   PROTEIN 7.3 G

Chicken breasts
with shiitake mushrooms

INGREDIENTS

6 chicken breast fillets
2 tablespoons peanut oil
1 onion, chopped
5 cm piece fresh root ginger,
  finely chopped
200 g (7 oz) shiitake mushrooms,
  stems removed and caps sliced
150 g (5 oz) baby button mushrooms
2 tablespoons dark soy sauce
300 ml (10 fl oz) chicken stock
200 ml (7 fl oz) dry white wine
350 g (11½ oz) zucchini (courgette),
  trimmed and sliced
fresh coriander, chopped to garnish
serves 4

PREPARATION TIME
15 minutes

COOKING TIME
50 minutes

1 Make 3 slashes in each chicken breast, using a sharp knife. Heat the oil in a large, heavy-based saucepan or frying pan with lid. Add the chicken and fry for 2–3 minutes on each side to brown. Remove to a plate.

2 Add the onion and ginger to the pan, fry until the onion has softened. Add both the mushrooms and the soy sauce and cook for a further 4–5 minutes.

3 Stir in the stock and wine and the zucchini slices. Bring to the boil then quickly turn down to a simmer. Return the chicken to the pan, cover and simmer for 15–20 minutes until chicken is cooked through. Sprinkle with fresh coriander and serve with rice or asian noodles.

NUTRITIONAL VALUE PER SERVE   FAT 4.5 G   CARBOHYDRATE 0.6 G   PROTEIN 13.5 G

Tangy tenderloins

INGREDIENTS

500 g (1 lb) chicken tenderloins
salt and pepper
olive oil spray
200 g (7 oz) sugar peas
425 g (14 oz) can baby corn, drained
$^1\!/_2$ cup (125 ml, 4 fl oz) apricot nectar
2 tablespoons sweet chilli sauce
2 tablespoons cider vinegar
serves 5

PREPARATION TIME
10 minutes

COOKING TIME
10 minutes

1 Flatten the tenderloins slightly and sprinkle with salt and pepper. Heat a heavy-based frying pan and spray lightly with oil spray. Add tenderloins and cook 2 minutes on each side. Remove from pan.

2 Add the sugar peas and stir around pan until they brighten in colour. Add the corn. Return the chicken to the pan and toss with the vegetables. In a bowl, combine the apricot nectar, sweet chilli sauce and vinegar. Pour over chicken and vegetables and heat through. Pile onto serving plates. Serve immediately.

NUTRITIONAL VALUE PER SERVE   FAT 3.2 G   CARBOHYDRATE 8.4 G   PROTEIN 9.4 G

Chicken rogan josh

INGREDIENTS

1 tablespoon vegetable oil
1 small green capsicum (pepper),
  thinly sliced
1 small red capsicum, thinly sliced
1 onion, thinly sliced
5 cm piece of fresh root ginger,
  finely chopped
2 cloves garlic, crushed
2 tablespoons garam masala
1 teaspoon paprika
1 teaspoon turmeric
1 teaspoon chilli powder
4 cardamom pods, crushed
salt to taste
8 chicken thigh fillets,
  each cut into 4 pieces
200 g (7 oz) natural yoghurt
400 g (13 oz) can chopped tomatoes
200 ml (7 fl oz) water
fresh coriander to garnish
mango chutney to serve
steamed rice to serve
serves 4

1 Heat the oil in a heavy-based frying pan. Add the capsicums, onion, ginger, garlic, spices and salt. Cover and fry over a low heat for 5 minutes or until the capsicums and onion have softened.

2 Add the chicken and stir until it changes colour. Stir in the yoghurt and cook gently for 5 minutes.

3 Stir in the tomatoes and water and bring to the boil. Reduce the heat, cover, and simmer for 30 minutes or until the chicken is tender, stirring occasionally and adding more water if the sauce becomes too dry. Sprinkle with coriander. Serve with steamed rice and mango chutney.

PREPARATION TIME
15 minutes

COOKING TIME
1 hour

NUTRITIONAL VALUE PER SERVE   FAT 4.9 G   CARBOHYDRATE 1 G   PROTEIN 16.6 G

Chicken rolls with an Indonesian flavour

INGREDIENTS

1 kg (2 lb) chicken thigh fillets
290 g (10 oz) can redang curry sauce
2 bananas
toothpicks
2 tablespoons vegetable oil
½ cup (125 ml, 4 fl oz) water
150 ml (5 fl oz) coconut milk
1 small pineapple, peeled and
  thinly sliced
freshly ground black pepper
2 tablespoons shredded coconut,
  toasted
steamed rice to serve
serves 4

PREPARATION TIME
15 minutes

COOKING TIME
45 minutes

1 Flatten the thigh fillets with a meat mallet to an even thinness. Spread each with a teaspoon of rendang curry sauce. Peel bananas and slit in half lengthwise then cut in half to make 4 pieces. Place a piece of banana in centre of each fillet and form into a roll. Fasten with a toothpick.

2 Heat oil in a wide-based saucepan and brown the rolls on all sides, a few at a time, removing rolls to a plate as they brown.

3 Drain all the oil from the saucepan and add rendang curry sauce and the water. Bring to the boil, turn down heat to a simmer and place in the chicken rolls. Cover and simmer 35 minutes, turning rolls once during cooking.

4 Remove rolls to a heated platter and keep hot. If sauce is thin, increase heat and reduce sauce to a thicker consistency. Reduce heat and stir in the coconut milk, simmer 2 minutes. Return rolls to the saucepan to reheat.

5 Saute the pineapple rings in a little butter until lightly coloured and grind over some black pepper. Arrange a slice of pineapple and a chicken roll on each plate, spoon sauce over the roll and sprinkle with a little toasted coconut. Accompany with steamed rice.

NUTRITIONAL VALUE PER SERVE   FAT 7.6 G   CARBOHYDRATE 4.8 G   PROTEIN 10.6 G

Spanish chicken with chorizo

INGREDIENTS

8 chicken pieces, thighs and
  drumsticks
2 tablespoons olive oil
1 onion, sliced
2 cloves garlic, crushed
1 red capsicum (pepper), deseeded
  and sliced
1 yellow capsicum, deseeded
  and sliced
2 teaspoons paprika
60 ml (2 fl oz) dry sherry
  or dry vermouth
400 g (13 oz) can chopped tomatoes
1 bay leaf
1 strip orange rind (zest), pared
  with a vegetable peeler
75 g (2½ oz) chorizo sausage, sliced
60 g (2 oz) pitted black olives
salt and black pepper
serves 4

PREPARATION TIME
15 minutes

COOKING TIME
1 hour

1 Place the chicken joints in a large non-stick frying pan and fry without oil for 5–8 minutes, turning occasionally, until golden. Remove the chicken and set aside, then wipe the pan clean with absorbent paper.

2 Add the oil to the pan and fry the onion, garlic and capsicums for 3–4 minutes, until softened. Return the chicken to the pan with the paprika, sherry or vermouth, tomatoes, bay leaf and orange rind. Bring to the boil. Simmer, covered, over a low heat for 35–40 minutes stirring occasionally, until the chicken is cooked through.

3 Add the chorizo and olives and simmer for a further 5 minutes to heat through, then season. Serve with crusty bread and a side salad.

NUTRITIONAL VALUE PER SERVE	FAT 5.3 G	CARBOHYDRATE 1.7 G	PROTEIN 12.5 G

Thai-spiced chicken with zucchini

INGREDIENTS

350 g (1–1½ oz) chicken breast fillets
1 tablespoon olive oil
1 clove garlic, finely chopped
2.5 cm fresh root ginger,
   finely chopped
1 small fresh red chilli, deseeded
   and finely chopped
1 tablespoon Thai seven-spice seasoning
1 red capsicum (pepper), deseeded
   and sliced
1 yellow capsicum, deseeded
   and sliced
2 zucchini (courgettes), thinly sliced
250 g (8 oz) can bamboo shoots, drained
2 tablespoons dry sherry or
   apple juice
1 tablespoon light soy sauce
black pepper
2 tablespoons chopped
   fresh coriander
extra coriander to garnish
hot noodles to serve
serves 4

1 With a sharp knife cut the chicken breasts into thin stir-fry strips.

2 Heat the oil in a non-stick wok or large frying pan. Add the garlic, ginger and chilli and stir-fry for 30 seconds to release the flavours. Add the chicken and Thai seasoning and stir-fry for 4 minutes or until the chicken has coloured. Add the capsicums and zucchini and stir-fry for 1–2 minutes, until slightly softened.

3 Stir in the bamboo shoots and stir-fry for another 2–3 minutes, until the chicken is cooked through and tender. Add the sherry or apple juice, soy sauce and black pepper and sizzle for 1–2 minutes. Remove from the heat and stir in the chopped fresh coriander. Garnish with more coriander and serve with hot noodles.

PREPARATION TIME
15 minutes

COOKING TIME
10 minutes

NUTRITIONAL VALUE PER SERVE   FAT 4.5 G   CARBOHYDRATE 1.8 G   PROTEIN 7.9 G

Crunchy drumsticks

INGREDIENTS

1 kg (2 lb) chicken drumsticks
2 tablespoons curry paste
60 g (2 oz) vinegar-flavoured
   corn chips or potato crisps
boiled rice or salad
mild chutney to serve
serves 4

1 Preheat oven to 180°C (350°F, gas mark 4). Rinse drumsticks and pat dry. With fingers rub the curry paste well into the skin of the drumsticks. Crush the corn chips or potato crisps and press onto the drumsticks.

2 Place on a rack over a shallow baking tray. Bake in a preheated oven for 35–40 minutes. Serve hot with boiled rice and a portion of chutney on the side. They may also be served cold with salad.

PREPARATION TIME
5 minutes

COOKING TIME
40 minutes

NUTRITIONAL VALUE PER SERVE   FAT **8.5** G   CARBOHYDRATE **2.9** G   PROTEIN **17.1** G

Easy apricot and mango chicken loaf

INGREDIENTS

700 g (1 lb 7 oz) chicken mince
50 g (2 oz) fresh breadcrumbs
90 g (3 oz) spring onions
   (green onions), chopped
   including green part
1 tablespoon finely chopped parsley
2 tablespoons diced dried apricots
1 tablespoon mango chutney
1 egg
1 teaspoon salt
1/4 teaspoon pepper
oil for greasing

Serves 6

1 Preheat oven to 180°C (350°F, gas mark 4). In a large bowl, place chicken mince. Add breadcrumbs, spring onions, parsley, apricots, chutney, egg, salt and pepper. With your hand, mix and knead mixture for 2–3 minutes to combine ingredients well and to give a fine texture.

2 Grease a 22 x 8 x 5 cm loaf tin with oil. Place in the mince mixture. Place in oven and bake for 50–55 minutes. To test insert skewer into centre and if clear juice appears it is cooked. If juice is a pink colour further cooking is required. Rest in the tin 10 minutes before turning out.

PREPARATION TIME
8 minutes

COOKING TIME
55 minutes, plus
10 minutes standing

NUTRITIONAL VALUE PER SERVE | FAT **7.7** G | CARBOHYDRATE **6.6** G | PROTEIN **15.7** G

Apricot-glazed chicken with savoury stuffing

INGREDIENTS

1.5 kg (3 lb) fresh chicken
½ lemon

apricot glaze
160 g (5½ oz) apricot jam
1 tablespoon soy sauce
1 tablespoon lemon juice
2 tablespoons white vinegar
1 tablespoon water

easy stuffing
3–4 rashers bacon, chopped
1 large onion, finely chopped
1 ³/₄ cups (350 g, 11½ oz) long-grain rice, rinsed
3 cups (750 ml, 24 fl oz) boiling water
2 teaspoons apricot glaze
2 teaspoons soy sauce
2 teaspoons mixed dried herbs
2 tablespoons chopped parsley
1 tablespoon flour, for gravy

serves 4

1 Preheat oven to 180°C (350°F, gas mark 5). Rinse out the chicken cavity, pat dry with paper towel and place the lemon half in the cavity. Tie drumsticks ends together with kitchen string or truss. In a saucepan, combine the apricot jam, soy sauce, lemon juice, vinegar and water and heat gently while stirring. Brush the chicken all over with glaze.

2 Place on an adjustable rack, breast-side down. Add a cup of water to the dish and place in the preheated oven for 40 minutes. Brush again with glaze and turn breast-side up, brush with glaze and continue to cook for 40–50 minutes more, until cooked when tested.

3 When chicken is placed in the oven, prepare the stuffing. Place all ingredients in a lidded casserole dish and place on a shelf in the oven under the chicken. Cook for 40 minutes then remove from oven and stand covered for 10 minutes.

4 When chicken is cooked, remove from dish and cover with foil to rest. Skim fat from roasting pan and add about 1 cup (250 ml, 8 fl oz) water to dissolve any cooked-on pan juices. Pour into a small saucepan. Add 1 tablespoon flour blended with a little water and stir until it thickens and boils. Carve chicken and serve with rice stuffing, gravy and vegetable accompaniments.

PREPARATION TIME
20 minutes

COOKING TIME
1 hour 30 minutes

| NUTRITIONAL VALUE PER SERVE | FAT 5.8 G | CARBOHYDRATE 16.9 G | PROTEIN 13.9 G |

Tandoori chicken

INGREDIENTS

2 (each about 1 kg, 2 lb)
   small chickens
3 tablespoons tandoori curry paste
200 g (7 oz) natural yoghurt
2 tablespoons lemon juice
2 tablespoons melted butter
$^1/_2$ cup (125 ml, 4 fl oz) water
lettuce for garnish
1 onion, cut into rings for garnish
1 tomato, cut into wedges for garnish
serves 4–6

PREPARATION TIME
15 minutes, plus
12 hours marinating

COOKING TIME
1 hour

1 Rinse chickens and pat dry. Make deep gashes in the thighs, drumsticks and breast with a sharp knife. Mix the tandoori curry paste, yoghurt, lemon juice and melted butter together.

2 In a large non-metallic dish, place chickens. Spread curry mixture all over the chickens, rubbing well into the gashes. Cover and refrigerate for 12 hours or more.

3 Preheat oven to 190°C (370°F, gas mark 5). Place chickens on a roasting rack in a baking dish, spoon over any of the remaining marinade. Add water to the base of the dish to prevent charring of pan juices.

4 Place chickens in the oven and cook for 1 hour. Baste with pan juices during cooking. Stand covered with foil 10 minutes before serving. Cut chickens into serving portions and place on platter lined with lettuce leaves. Garnish with onion rings and tomato.

NUTRITIONAL VALUE PER SERVE	FAT 11.6 G	CARBOHYDRATE 0.7 G	PROTEIN 16.5 G

Roasted herb stuffed chicken

INGREDIENTS

4 chicken breasts, on the bone
  with skin on

herb stuffing

2 tablespoons thick natural yoghurt
1 clove garlic, crushed
1 teaspoon olive oil
2 tablespoons finely chopped mint
2 tablespoons finely chopped
  flat-leaf parsley
2 tablespoons finely
  chopped oregano
2 tablespoons finely chopped thyme
2 tablespoons finely chopped dill
2 spring onions (green onions),
  finely chopped
salt and finely ground black pepper

serves 4–6

PREPARATION TIME
15 minutes, plus
1½hours
refrigeration

COOKING TIME
20 minutes

1 In a small bowl, combine together all the herb stuffing ingredients and mix well.

2 Using your finger tips, scoop up a quarter of the mixture and gently push under the skin of the chicken. Run your fingers over the skin to smooth the stuffing out. Attach skin with a toothpick to side of breast if needed. Repeat with the remaining pieces. Cover, and refrigerate for 1½ hours.

3 Pre-heat the oven to 180°C (350°F, gas mark 4). Place the chicken on a roasting rack and cook in the oven for 15–20 minutes.

4 Remove to a chopping board. Remove bone carefully and cut into thick diagonal slices. Skim fat from pan juices and pour over the chicken.

NUTRITIONAL VALUE PER SERVE	FAT 9.9 G	CARBOHYDRATE 0.3 G	PROTEIN 18.7 G

Roast chicken with basil and red onion

INGREDIENTS

1.5 kg (3 lb) chicken
1 handful fresh basil leaves
120 ml (4 fl oz) extra virgin
  olive oil
juice of ½ lemon
sea salt and freshly ground
  black pepper
4 medium red onions
rind (zest) of ½ lemon,
  grated
1 garlic clove, crushed
serves 4

1　Preheat the oven to 190°C (375°F, gas mark 5). Place the chicken in a roasting pan. Gently work the skin away from the flesh with your fingers and tuck about 6–7 basil leaves under the breast skin. Place the remaining basil in a liquidiser with the olive oil, lemon juice and seasoning and whiz until smooth. Brush the chicken with half the basil oil. Place in preheated oven and roast for 40 minutes.

2　Peel the onion and slice off the root end to give a flat base. Make four cuts, in a criss-cross shape, across the top of each onion to come only halfway down, so the onions open slightly. Combine the lemon rind with the garlic and sprinkle over the onions.

3　Add the onions to the chicken in the pan and brush well with some of the basil oil. Brush the remaining oil over the chicken and cook for a further 40 minutes or until cooked through. Cover and allow the chicken to rest for 10 minutes before carving.

PREPARATION TIME
20 minutes, plus
10 minutes resting

COOKING TIME
1 hour 10 minutes

NUTRITIONAL VALUE PER SERVE　　　FAT 13.3 G　　　CARBOHYDRATE 1.2 G　　　PROTEIN 14.2 G

Oven-baked parmesan chicken

INGREDIENTS

60 g (2 oz) fresh breadcrumbs,
  made from country-style bread
75 g (3 oz) parmesan, finely grated
2 spring onions (green onions),
  finely chopped
finely grated rind (zest)
  and juice of ½ lemon
4 tablespoons butter, melted
sea salt and freshly ground
  black pepper
4 chicken breast fillets
2 tablespoons chopped fresh parsley
serves 4

1 Preheat the oven to 190°C (375°F, gas mark 5). In a small bowl, mix together the breadcrumbs, parmesan, spring onions, lemon rind, butter, salt and pepper.

2 Divide the mixture between the chicken breasts and using a fork, press the mixture on top, to form an even coat.

3 Transfer the chicken breasts to a greased shallow oven tray and bake for 20 minutes. Remove the chicken and keep warm. Add the lemon juice and parsley to the buttery juices in the tray and mix well. Pour these juices over the chicken and serve immediately.

PREPARATION TIME
15 minutes

COOKING TIME
20 minutes

NUTRITIONAL VALUE PER SERVE	FAT 9.9 G	CARBOHYDRATE 2.6 G	PROTEIN 20 G

Chicken breasts with mushrooms and cream

INGREDIENTS

2 tablespoons butter
1 clove garlic, crushed
125 g (4 oz) chestnut mushrooms,
    finely chopped
125 g (4 oz) chestnut mushrooms,
    sliced
salt and black pepper
1 tablespoon chopped fresh
    flat-leaf parsley
1 tablespoon chopped fresh tarragon
4 large chicken breast fillets
150 ml (5 fl oz) chicken stock
150 ml (5 fl oz) sparkling or dry
    white wine
150 ml (5 fl oz) whipping cream
fresh flat-leaf parsley to garnish
serves 4

PREPARATION TIME
20 minutes, plus
10 minutes cooling

COOKING TIME
45 minutes

1 Melt half the butter in a frying pan. Add the garlic and chopped mushrooms, reserving the sliced mushrooms. Season and cook, stirring, over a high heat for 5 minutes or until softened. Place into a bowl, stir in the parsley and tarragon and leave to cool for 10 minutes.

2 Make a slit down the centre of each chicken breast, then insert the tip of a knife into either side of the slit to open it out into a pocket. Place the chicken in a baking dish and spoon the mushroom mixture into the pockets.

3 Preheat the oven to 180°C (350°F, gas mark 4). Melt the remaining butter in a frying pan. Add the sliced mushrooms, salt and pepper and cook over a high heat for 3 minutes. Add the stock, wine and cream and bring to the boil. Simmer for 10 minutes or until thickened slightly. Pour over the chicken, cover with foil and cook for 20–25 minutes, basting halfway through. To serve, spoon the sauce over the chicken and garnish with parsley.

NUTRITIONAL VALUE PER SERVE   FAT 6.8 G   CARBOHYDRATE 0.4 G   PROTEIN 15.3 G

Glossary

Al dente: Italian term to describe pasta and rice that are cooked until tender but still firm to the bite.

Bake blind: to bake pastry cases without their fillings. Line the raw pastry case with greaseproof paper and fill with raw rice or dried beans to prevent collapsed sides and puffed base. Remove paper and fill 5 minutes before completion of cooking time.

Baste: to spoon hot cooking liquid over food at intervals during cooking to moisten and flavour it.

Beat: to make a mixture smooth with rapid and regular motions using a spatula, wire whisk or electric mixer; to make a mixture light and smooth by enclosing air.

Beurre manié: equal quantities of butter and flour mixed together to a smooth paste and stirred bit by bit into a soup, stew or sauce while on the heat to thicken. Stop adding when desired thickness results.

Bind: to add egg or a thick sauce to hold ingredients together when cooked.

Blanch: to plunge some foods into boiling water for less than a minute and immediately plunge into iced water. This is to brighten the colour of some vegetables; to remove skin from tomatoes and nuts.

Blend: to mix 2 or more ingredients thoroughly together; do not confuse with blending in an electric blender.

Boil: to cook in a liquid brought to boiling point and kept there.

Boiling point: when bubbles rise continually and break over the entire surface of the liquid, reaching a temperature of 100°C (212°F). In some cases food is held at this high temperature for a few seconds then heat is turned to low for slower cooking. See simmer.

Bouquet garni: a bundle of several herbs tied together with string for easy removal, placed into pots of stock, soups and stews for flavour. A few sprigs of fresh thyme, parsley and bay leaf are used. Can be purchased in sachet form for convenience.

Caramelise: to heat sugar in a heavy-based pan until it liquefies and develops a caramel colour. Vegetables such as blanched carrots and sautéed onions may be sprinkled with sugar and caramelised.

Chill: to place in the refrigerator or stir over ice until cold.

Clarify: to make a liquid clear by removing sediments and impurities. To melt fat and remove any sediment.

Coat: to dust or roll food items in flour to cover the surface before the food is cooked. Also, to coat in flour, egg and breadcrumbs.

Cool: to stand at room temperature until some or all heat is removed, e.g. cool a little, cool completely.

Cream: to make creamy and fluffy by working the mixture with the back of a wooden spoon, usually refers to creaming butter and sugar or margarine. May also be creamed with an electric mixer.

Croutons: small cubes of bread, toasted or fried, used as an addition to salads or as a garnish to soups and stews.

Crudite: raw vegetable sticks served with a dipping sauce.

Crumb: to coat foods in flour, egg and breadcrumbs to form a protective coating for foods which are fried. Also adds flavour, texture and enhances appearance.

Cube: to cut into small pieces with six even sides, e.g. cubes of meat.

Cut in: to combine fat and flour using 2 knives scissor fashion or with a pastry blender, to make pastry.

Deglaze: to dissolve dried out cooking juices left on the base and sides of a roasting dish or frying pan. Add a little water, wine or stock, scrape and stir over heat until dissolved. Resulting liquid is used to make a flavoursome gravy or added to a sauce or casserole.

Degrease: to skim fat from the surface of cooking liquids, e.g. stocks, soups, casseroles.

Dice: to cut into small cubes.

Dredge: to heavily coat with icing sugar, sugar, flour or cornflour.

Dressing: a mixture added to completed dishes to add moisture and flavour, e.g. salads, cooked vegetables.

Drizzle: to pour in a fine thread-like stream moving over a surface.

Egg wash: beaten egg with milk or water used to brush over pastry, bread dough or biscuits to give a sheen and golden brown colour.

Essence: a strong flavouring liquid, usually made by distillation. Only a few drops are needed to flavour.

Fillet: a piece of prime meat, fish or poultry which is boneless or has all bones removed.

Flake: to separate cooked fish into flakes, removing any bones and skin, using 2 forks.

Flame: to ignite warmed alcohol over food or to pour into a pan with food, ignite then serve.

Flute: to make decorative indentations around the pastry rim before baking.

Fold in: combining of a light, whisked or creamed mixture with other ingredients. Add a portion of the other ingredients at a time and mix using a gentle circular motion, over and under the mixture so that air will not be lost. Use a silver spoon or spatula.

Glaze: to brush or coat food with a liquid that will give the finished product a glossy appearance, and on baked products, a golden brown colour.

Grease: to rub the surface of a metal or heatproof dish with oil or fat, to prevent the food from sticking.

Herbed butter: softened butter mixed with finely chopped fresh herbs and re-chilled. Used to serve on grilled meats and fish.

Hors D'Oeuvre: small savoury foods served as an appetiser, popularly known today as 'finger food'.

Infuse: to steep foods in a liquid until the liquid absorbs their flavour.

Joint: to cut poultry and game into serving pieces by dividing at the joint.

Julienne: to cut some food, e.g. vegetables and processed meats into fine strips the length of matchsticks. Used for inclusion in salads or as a garnish to cooked dishes.

Knead: to work a yeast dough in a pressing, stretching and folding motion with the heel of the hand until smooth and elastic to develop the gluten strands. Non-yeast doughs should be lightly and quickly handled as gluten development is not desired.

Line: to cover the inside of a baking tin with paper for the easy removal of the cooked product from the baking tin.

Macerate: to stand fruit in a syrup, liqueur or spirit to give added flavour.

Marinade: a flavoured liquid, into which food is placed for some time to give it flavour and to tenderise. Marinades include an acid ingredient such as vinegar or wine, oil and seasonings.

Mask: to evenly cover cooked food portions with a sauce, mayonnaise or savoury jelly.

Pan-fry: to fry foods in a small amount of fat or oil, sufficient to coat the base of the pan.

Parboil: to boil until partially cooked. The food is then finished by some other method.

Pare: to peel the skin from vegetables and fruit. Peel is the popular term but pare is the name given to the knife used; paring knife.

Pith: the white lining between the rind and flesh of oranges, grapefruit and lemons.

Pit: to remove stones or seeds from olives, cherries, dates.

Pitted: the olives, cherries, dates etc. with the stone removed, e.g. purchase pitted dates.

Poach: to simmer gently in enough hot liquid to almost cover the food so shape will be retained.

Pound: to flatten meats with a meat mallet; to reduce to a paste or small particles with a mortar and pestle.

Simmer: to cook in liquid just below boiling point at about 96°C (205°F) with small bubbles rising gently to the surface.

Skim: to remove fat or froth from the surface of simmering food.

Stock: the liquid produced when meat, poultry, fish or vegetables have been simmered in water to extract the flavour. Used as a base for soups, sauces, casseroles etc. Convenience stock products are available.

Sweat: to cook sliced onions or vegetables, in a small amount of butter in a covered pan over low heat, to soften them and release flavour without colouring.

Conversions

Measurements differ from country to country, so it's important to understand what the differences are. This Measurements Guide gives you simple 'at-a-glance' information for using the recipes in this book, wherever you may be.

Cooking is not an exact science – minor variations in measurements won't make a difference to your cooking.

EQUIPMENT

There is a difference in the size of measuring cups used internationally, but the difference is minimal (only 2–3 teaspoons). We use the Australian standard metric measurements in our recipes:

1 teaspoon ....5 ml   1 tablespoon....20 ml

1/2 cup......125 ml   1 cup.....250 ml

4 cups...1 litre

Measuring cups come in sets of one cup (250 ml), 1/2 cup (125 ml), 1/3 cup (80 ml) and 1/4 cup (60 ml). Use these for measuring liquids and certain dry ingredients.

Measuring spoons come in a set of four and should be used for measuring dry and liquid ingredients.

When using cup or spoon measures always make them level (unless the recipe indicates otherwise).

DRY VERSUS WET INGREDIENTS

While this system of measures is consistent for liquids, it's more difficult to quantify dry ingredients. For instance, one level cup equals: 200 g of brown sugar; 210 g of castor sugar; and 110 g of icing sugar.

When measuring dry ingredients such as flour, don't push the flour down or shake it into the cup. It is best just to spoon the flour in until it reaches the desired amount. When measuring liquids use a clear vessel indicating metric levels.

Always use medium eggs (55–60 g) when eggs are required in a recipe.

OVEN

Your oven should always be at the right temperature before placing the food in it to be cooked. Note that if your oven doesn't have a fan you may need to cook food for a little longer.

MICROWAVE

It is difficult to give an exact cooking time for microwave cooking. It is best to watch what you are cooking closely to monitor its progress.

STANDING TIME

Many foods continue to cook when you take them out of the oven or microwave. If a recipe states that the food needs to 'stand' after cooking, be sure not to overcook the dish.

CAN SIZES

The can sizes available in your supermarket or grocery store may not be the same as specified in the recipe. Don't worry if there is a small variation in size – it's unlikely to make a difference to the end result.

dry		liquids	
metric (grams)	imperial (ounces)	metric (millilitres)	imperial (fluid ounces)
		30 ml	1 fl oz
30 g	1 oz	60 ml	2 fl oz
60 g	2 oz	90 ml	3 fl oz
90 g	3 oz	100 ml	3 1/2 fl oz
100 g	3 1/2 oz	125 ml	4 fl oz
125 g	4 oz	150 ml	5 fl oz
150 g	5 oz	190 ml	6 fl oz
185 g	6 oz	250 ml	8 fl oz
200 g	7 oz	300 ml	10 fl oz
250 g	8 oz	500 ml	16 fl oz
280 g	9 oz	600 ml	20 fl oz (1 pint)*
315 g	10 oz	1000 ml (1 litre)	32 fl oz
330 g	11 oz		
370 g	12 oz		
400 g	13 oz		
440 g	14 oz		
470 g	15 oz		
500 g	16 oz (1 lb)		
750 g	24 oz (1 1/2 lb)		
1000 g (1 kg)	32 oz (2 lb)	*Note: an American pint is 16 fl oz.	

cooking temperatures	°C (celsius)	°F (fahrenheit)	gas mark
very slow	120	250	1/2
slow	150	300	2
moderately slow	160	315	2–3
moderate	180	350	4
moderate hot	190	375	5
	200	400	6
hot	220	425	7
very hot	230	450	8
	240	475	9
	250	500	10

Index

Essential COOKING SERIES

COMPREHENSIVE, STEP BY STEP COOKING

Essential COOKING SERIES
COMPREHENSIVE, STEP BY STEP COOKING
Baking

Essential COOKING SERIES
COMPREHENSIVE, STEP BY STEP COOKING
Chicken Meals

Essential COOKING SERIES
COMPREHENSIVE, STEP BY STEP COOKING
Salads & Greens

Essential COOKING SERIES
COMPREHENSIVE, STEP BY STEP COOKING
Soups & Hors D'Oeuvres

Essential COOKING SERIES
COMPREHENSIVE, STEP BY STEP COOKING
Meat Dishes

Essential COOKING SERIES
COMPREHENSIVE, STEP BY STEP COOKING
Finger Food

Essential COOKING SERIES
COMPREHENSIVE, STEP BY STEP COOKING
Pasta Dishes

Essential COOKING SERIES
COMPREHENSIVE, STEP BY STEP COOKING
Grilling & Barbecuing

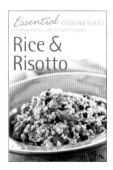

Essential COOKING SERIES
COMPREHENSIVE, STEP BY STEP COOKING
Rice & Risotto

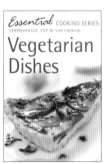

Essential COOKING SERIES
COMPREHENSIVE, STEP BY STEP COOKING
Vegetarian Dishes

Essential COOKING SERIES
COMPREHENSIVE, STEP BY STEP COOKING
Asian Dishes

Essential COOKING SERIES
COMPREHENSIVE, STEP BY STEP COOKING
Stir-Fry